# The 1920s

## Britain in Pictures

# The 1920s

## Britain in Pictures

PA Photos

AMMONITE
PRESS

First Published 2008 by
Ammonite Press
an imprint of AE Publications Ltd,
166 High Street, Lewes, East Sussex BN7 1XU

Text copyright Ammonite Press
Images copyright PA Photos
Copyright in the work Ammonite Press

ISBN 978-1-906672-08-9

British Cataloguing in Publication Data. A catalogue
record of this book is available from the British Library.

Editor: Paul Richardson
Picture research: PA Photos
Design: Gravemaker + Scott

Colour reproduction by GMC Reprographics
Printed by Colorprint, China

Page 2: The Prince of Wales
kicking off a football match
between Tottenham Hotspur
and Fulham.
**14th May, 1921**

Page 5: A dustman at work
in Kentish Town.
**13th July, 1925**

Page 6: Traffic in The
Strand, Central London.
**11th October, 1929**

# Introduction

The archives of PA Photos yield a unique insight into Britain's recent past. Thanks to the science of photography we can view the 20th Century more accurately than any that came before, but it is thanks to news photography, and in particular the great news agency that is The Press Association, that we are able now to witness the events that made up life in Britain, not so long ago.

It is easy, looking back, to imagine a past neatly partitioned into clearly defined periods and dominated by landmarks: wars, political upheaval and economic trends. But the archive tells a different story: alongside the major events that constitute formal history are found the smaller things that had equal – if not greater – significance for ordinary people at the time. And while the photographers were working for that moment's news rather than posterity, the camera is an undiscriminating eye that records everything in its view: to modern eyes it is often the backgrounds of these pictures, not their intended subjects, that provide the greatest fascination. Likewise it is revealed that Britain does not pass neatly from one period to another.

The years between 1st January, 1920 and 31st December, 1929 should, by rights, be overshadowed by the terrible suffering and loss of life so recently borne in the Great War. Yet while memorials to those who died are prominent throughout the decade, the atmosphere is one of great energy, optimism, achievement and enjoyment – almost hedonism. Perhaps those who survived were driven to savour life all the more. Records fell like skittles as fearless motor and aviation pioneers forced technological leaps and bounds to be made; sportsmen displayed ambition and idealism rather than professionalism – the 'Chariots of Fire' Olympics fell in these years – and the doings of the arts & entertainment industries were on everyone's lips.

It was the first age of celebrity, in that peculiarly modern sense. Sportsmen, aviators, royalty, actors, military officers, millionaires, racing drivers... all merged and mingled as a glittering elite. Counts and well-born ladies raced at Brooklands, noblemen won medals at the Olympics, cabaret artistes won fortunes in the casinos, actresses married millionaires and army officers crossed oceans in flimsy aircraft.

Given what the country had been through, and would go through again all too soon, who can blame them?

Slum children playing in the
streets outside their homes
in Laursa Place, Shoreditch,
London.
**1920**

A rush for trams on the Victoria Embankment in London during the railway strike.
**1920**

Scottish lasses chase the herring, and the work, south to Scarborough, North Yorkshire. Here three girls carry a double-handful of 'caller herring' which are about to be pickled in brine.
**1920**

Sir Ernest Cassel shooting at Newmarket. Having arrived penniless in Liverpool in 1869, the Prussian-born merchant banker, art collector, racehorse breeder and philanthropist became a friend of King Edward VII, Asquith and the young Winston Churchill. At his death in 1921, his estate was valued at £6m.

**1920**

Harold MacMillan on his
wedding day with his bride,
the former Lady Dorothy
Cavendish, daughter of the
9th Duke of Cavendish.
**1920**

King George V passing
down the lines of heroes
at a garden party for
Victoria Cross awardees at
Buckingham Palace. On the
right is Prince Henry.
**1920**

Bombardier Billy Wells.
The boxer later became
the second 'man with the
gong', seen at the start of
films made by the Rank
Organisation.
**1920**

Aviators Captain G de Haviland (L) and Alan J Cobham.
**1920**

New signaling apparatus
at Victoria Station, London.
The Chatham Express is
leaving Victoria Station with
the signal shown in its new
vertical position, indicating
'all clear'.
**5th January, 1920**

(L-R) W J A 'Dave' Davies
and Cecil Kershaw, United
Services. Rugby Union –
United Services v English
Public Schools.
**1st April, 1920**

Abe Waddington, England.
**1st April, 1920**

Welterweight Ted 'Kid' Lewis.
**1st April, 1920**

Miss Corderey, who
competed in the Easter
Monday Handicap,
Brooklands, at which motor
racing recommenced in 1920
having been suspended for
the Great War.
**5th April, 1920**

Jimmy Wilde, boxer.
**1st May, 1920**

Harry Vardon, of golf's
'Great Triumvirate'.
**1st May, 1920**

Mlle Suzanne Lenglen,
winner of 31 lawn tennis
Grand Slam titles from
1914 to 1926, in play at
Wimbledon.
**16th June, 1920**

Miss Maggie Williams, a former parlourmaid to Mrs Greenwood, one of the witnesses at the Greenwood Poisoning inquest.
**17th June, 1920**

The arrest of Mr Greenwood. He is seen here leaving Kidwelly Police Station for Llanelly, where he will be charged with the murder, by poisoning, of his first wife.
**17th June, 1920**

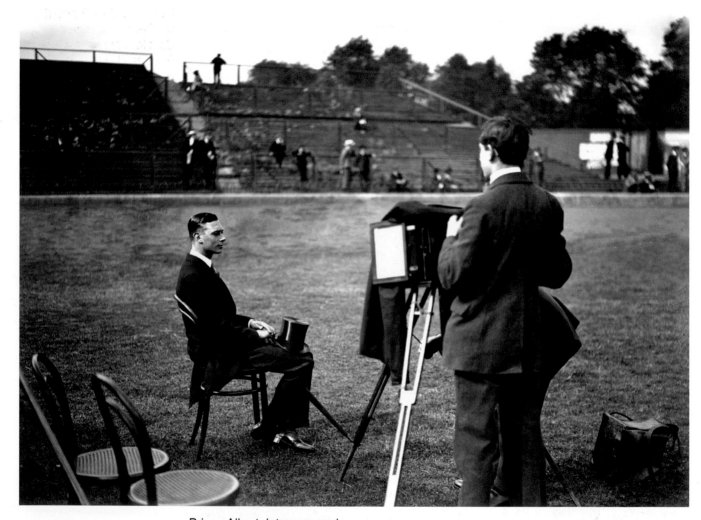

Prince Albert, later crowned
as King George VI following
his brother Edward's
abdication, poses for his
photograph at the Civil
Service Annual Athletic
Sports at Stamford Bridge.
**19th June, 1920**

Film stars Mary Pickford and her new husband Douglas Fairbanks arrive at Southampton.
**21st June, 1920**

The Countess of Wilton
driving during the Ladies'
Parliamentary Golf at
Edgware.
**25th June, 1920**

French tennis players Rene Lacoste and Suzanne Lenglen in play at the International Tennis Party at Roehampton.
**3rd July, 1920**

The King, Queen and Princess Mary visit the site of the Scottish National War memorial at Edinburgh Castle. The Duke of Atholl is making an explanation on the subject of the apex of the Castle.

**8th July, 1920**

New on the market, a
design patented by Mr P
T Stanley and Mr S Adler.
Push buttons on the motor
car's steering wheel operate
directional indicators.
**8th July, 1920**

The exterior of Olympia, built
in 1886, pictured in 1920.
**1st August, 1920**

King George V, Queen
Mary (C), Princess Mary
(R) and the Duke of York
photographed with the crew
of the 'Britannia'.
**4th August, 1920**

Count Zborowski's huge 23 litre Maybach aero-engined racer 'Chitty Bang Bang', which has streamlined bodywork allowing a speed of 120mph. This was to be the first of three cars bearing the name, derived not from the car's noise but from a bawdy Great War soldiers' song.

**14th August, 1920**

Albert Hill of Great Britain winning the heat in the 800 metres at the Olympic Games in Antwerp. He went on to win the gold medal.
**17th August, 1920**

Britain's victory over Belgium in the Water Polo final at the Olympic Games. The team captain (with ball) was Paul Radmilovic. The rest of the team, in no order, were: Charles Sydney Smith, Charles Bugbee, Noel Purcell, Christopher Jones, William Peacock and William Henry Dean.

**28th August, 1920**

A gentleman – one P L
Hamlin – poses with a rag
and bone man in London.
**1st October, 1920**

Joyce Wethered, held to be
Britain's best woman golfer,
at Portrush.
**1st October, 1920**

Miners' safety lamps are stored between shifts at the Lewis Merthyr Colliery, Pontypridd near Cardiff.
**1st October, 1920**

Prince Henry (with shotgun),
third son of King George
V and Queen Mary, goes
shooting at Ailton Hall in
Salisbury.
**2nd October, 1920**

A man and girl at work with
an ordinary cigarette making
machine, which produces
7,000,000 cigarettes a
month or 650 every minute,
at Messrs Carreras Arcadia
Works.
**7th October, 1920**

Police use a Ford motor
car to regulate slow-moving
traffic in the East End of
London.
**12th October, 1920**

Prince Albert, The Duke
of York, during a visit to
the children's ward at the
Homeopathic Hospital on
Great Ormond Street.
**4th November, 1920**

Facing page: On Armistice
Day, the body of an
unidentified soldier taken
from the battlefields of the
Great War was interred in
the Tomb of the Unknown
Soldier in Westminster
Abbey. Here the coffin rests
before the ceremony.
**9th November, 1920**

The King arriving at
Westminster Abbey for
the burial of the unknown
soldier.
**11th November, 1920**

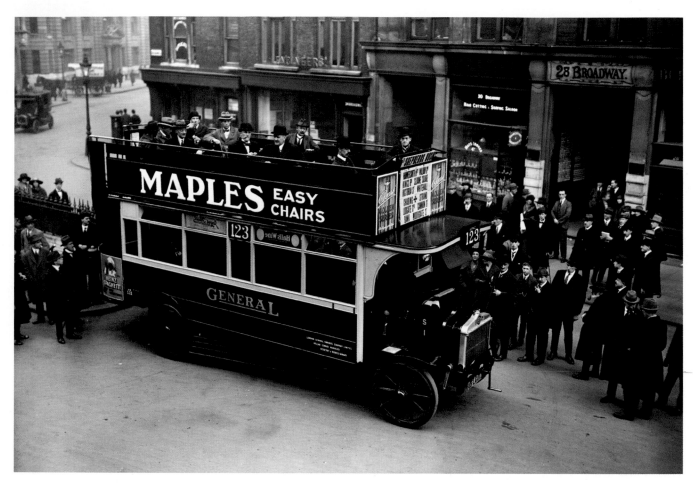

The 'K' type of motor bus.
**16th November, 1920**

Action from the final Varsity
Match played at Queen's
Club.
**6th December, 1920**

An ice cream vendor and his customers on the streets on London.
**3rd January, 1921**

Facing page: Three of the competitors in the International Beauty Show at Folkstone: (L-R) Miss Fidge (Italy), Violet Pout (England), Berthy Egli (Spain).
**1921**

'Shaun Spadah' ridden by
F B Rees wins the Grand
National. This was the only
horse not to fall during the
whole race, although three
others out of 35 runners also
finished the course after
being remounted.
**19th March, 1921**

Count Zborowski's aero-
engined racer and the 8
hp 'G.N.' afford a striking
contrast during tuning up
operations at Brooklands.
**26th March, 1921**

A Royal Defence Force
sentry at Somerset House,
during the strike crisis.
**1st April, 1921**

King George V, Queen Mary and Princess Mary in the paddock after the Prince of Wales (L) was successful in his first ride under National Hunt rules.

**1st April, 1921**

Scotland v England
International at Hampden
Park: the England team
group.
**9th April, 1921**

Lady Warrender out for a
drive in the park with Audrey
James at the wheel.
**14th April, 1921**

P G H Fender during bowling practice at Surrey's training at The Oval.
**28th April, 1921**

Facing page: Crown Prince Hirohito of Japan (plumed hat) landing at Portsmouth during his visit to England. Later that year the Prince was to become Regent of Japan.
**9th May, 1921**

Winston Churchill
during a game of polo at
Roehampton.
**18th May, 1921**

The very latest in bathing caps, costumes and wraps as designed by Harrods, modelled in this charming Margate snapshot featured in 'Eve's Film Review', Pathe Frere's weekly film review for women.
**20th May, 1921**

The Prince of Wales at the English Fair and Fete at Plymouth.
**20th May, 1921**

'Humorist' (second L) with Steve Donoghue up, comes home to win The Epsom Derby.
**1st June, 1921**

Boxing competitions
between women have been
exciting interest.
**11th June, 1921**

Queen Alexandra leaving
Marlborough House for her
drive through London on
Alexandra Day.
**22nd June, 1921**

Lloyd George at the unveiling of a war memorial in Thame. In his speech he said; 'If there is another war it will be terrible beyond thought'.
**30th July, 1921**

Facing page: The British Empire reached an accord with the Irish revolutionary group Sinn Fein; Ireland was to become a free state. Eamon De Valera and his party on the Irish boat at Holyhead (L-R) R C Barton, Eamon De Valera, Count Plunkett, Arthur Griffiths and Austin Stack.
**12th July, 1921**

Ballet dancer Anna Pavlova
takes part in the Cowdray
Polo Finals.
**30th July, 1921**

The mass of tangled
wreckage of the airship R38
(also known as ZRII) is seen
at low tide in the Humber
Estuary. 27 Britons and 16
Americans were killed when
the airship exploded during a
trial flight over Hull.
**25th August, 1921**

Edith Kelly Gould, who married American multi-millionaire Frank Jay Gould in Edinburgh in 1910, dancing in 'Pins and Needles'. She is reputed to have to highest 'kick' in the world.

**1st September, 1921**

The King's three sons, kilted,
at the Braemar Gathering:
(L-R) the Prince of Wales,
the Earl of Athlone, the Duke
of York and Prince Henry.
**9th September, 1921**

Sitting on the rail of the Olympic, Charlie Chaplin chats to a young admirer.
**10th September, 1921**

Charlie Chaplin addressing
the crowd outside the Ritz
Hotel, where he is staying.
**10th September, 1921**

Herriet Hammond with
Fatty Arbuckle on the set
of 'Should A Man Marry' in
London.
**20th September, 1921**

The Queen Mother when she was Lady Elizabeth Bowes-Lyon with her father, the Earl of Strathmore.
**29th September, 1921**

During his visit to London, Charlie Chaplin flew to Paris from Croydon. Here he is seen putting on his flying kit.
**5th October, 1921**

Count Zborowski in his
Aston Martin for the Light
Car Derby at Brooklands.
**21st October, 1921**

The Prince of Wales (later King Edward VIII, then the Duke of Windsor) visits the Mediterranean island and British naval base of Malta. Here crowds wait on the quayside and in harbour boats to see the Prince.
**8th November, 1921**

Lloyd George and Winston Churchill lay wreaths at the War Cenotaph, London, on Armistice Day.
**11th November, 1921**

The Maharajah Regent (R),
Sir Pertub Singh, returning
from the palace at Jodphur
with a British official after his
visit to the Prince of Wales,
touring India.
**29th November, 1921**

Sir J M Barrie (with stick)
the eminent playwright best
known for 'Peter Pan', at the
Charing Cross coffee stall.
**2nd December, 1921**

King George V and Queen
Maud of Norway were
present at King's Cross
to greet King Haakon of
Norway and Prince Olaf on
their arrival. (L-R) Princess
Victoria, King George V,
The King of Norway, Queen
Maud of Norway and Prince
Olaf.
**20th December, 1921**

The Victoria Memorial Hall
in Calcutta, built in memory
of the late Queen Victoria,
a magnificent building of
marble which cost 67 million
rupees to build and which
took 16 years to construct.
The foundation stone was
laid in 1905.
**28th December, 1921**

A A Milne with his son in the nursery where Winnie the Pooh was born.
**1922**

Sir J M Barrie with legendary
actress Ellen Terry at St.
Andrews University.
1922

Signor Cislafhi with his one wheel motorcycle, capable of speeds up to 40mph. Trials proved successful, unlike subsequent marketing of the vehicle.
**1922**

On tour in the East, the
Prince of Wales (L) plays
polo in Bangalore.
**8th January, 1922**

The West Norfolk Foxhounds met at Sandringham and before the hounds moved off, a presentation was made to Princess Mary as a wedding gift, subscribed by members of the hunt. Queen Alexandra chats to Princess Mary.

**9th January, 1922**

The scene inside the oak room at the Mansion House, Dublin, during the formal Ratification of the Irish Treaty. Mr Griffiths is seated on the left (centre, wearing glasses) and Republican Michael Collins is facing the speaker.
**16th January, 1922**

The Prince of Wales at the unveiling of the Edward VII Memorial in Delhi.
**15th February, 1922**

Facing page: At the railway station the Prince of Wales climbs the staircase to take his seat in the howdah of the Royal Elephant. The Prince is followed by the Maharajah of Gwalior.
**8th February, 1922**

A successful flight was
made, near Paris, by this
'Helicopter' invented by M de
Pescara.
**18th February, 1922**

The Prince of Wales in uniform of the 35th and 36th Jacobs Horse of which he is the Colonel in Chief.
**20th February, 1922**

Princess Mary and Viscount
Lascelles with King George
V, Queen Mary (R) and
Queen Alexandra after their
Royal Wedding ceremony at
Westminster Abbey.
**28th February, 1922**

The Prince of Wales is carried through the streets of Hong Kong to Government House.

**6th April, 1922**

The new White Star Liner
'Majestic', the largest ship in
the world.
**10th April, 1922**

The Prince of Wales and two
of his companions dressed
in traditional Japanese
costume whilst on board
HMS Renown sailing from
Hong Kong to Japan.
**20th April, 1922**

Alexander Ramsey, the
grandson of the 13th Earl of
Dalhousie, stands at salute
with his nurse under the
Walls of Windsor Castle
whilst waiting to watch the
Changing of the Guard.
**20th April, 1922**

Waterloo Station.
**25th April, 1922**

King George V (R) inspecting the graves of British soldiers killed during the fighting in the infamous Ypres Salient. To the left can be seen Field Marshal Sir Douglas Haig, Commander of the British Army on the Western Front.
**12th May, 1922**

P G H Fender, the Surrey
Captain, was in remarkable
form scoring 185 runs before
he was caught by S Fry,
son of the famous C B Fry.
Surrey v Hampshire.
**13th May, 1922**

The Honourable G A
Egerton, in the fourth race
at Brooklands, driving a
Bentley.
**3rd June, 1922**

Queen Alexandra with
Princess Victoria driving
through London in
connection with Alexandra
Day.
**21st June, 1922**

English golf legend James Braid (C) meets up with four American Open entrants during a practice session: (L-R) Robert Gardner, Francis Ouimet, Braid, Jess Sweetser and Harrison Johnston.
**1st July, 1922**

The bride, Edwina Ashley,
and groom at the wedding of
Lord Louis Mountbatten at
Brook House, London.
**18th July, 1922**

Former actress Lily Langtry picking fruit in a garden. She achieved notoriety as the mistress of King Edward VII.
**1st September, 1922**

A J Cobham, who reached Croydon third in the Great Air Race around Britain.
**9th September, 1922**

Music hall comedian Sir
Harry Lauder leaving with
Lady Lauder for a tour
around the world.
**16th September, 1922**

Lord and Lady Mountbatten pictured before leaving for America.

**27th September, 1922**

(L-R) Arsenal manager Leslie Knighton, captain Bill Blyth and goalkeeper Steve Dunn make their way to the FA Inquiry into a controversial match between Arsenal and Tottenham Hotspur when two players were sent off during a particularly vicious and bitter game.

**5th October, 1922**

Freddy Bywaters arriving at court during the Bywaters-Thompson case, in which he was found gulty and hanged, as was his lover Edith Thompson, for the murder of Percy Thompson. It is now believed that Edith was innocent of the murder. A million people signed an unsuccessful petition for the couple's reprieve.
**6th October, 1922**

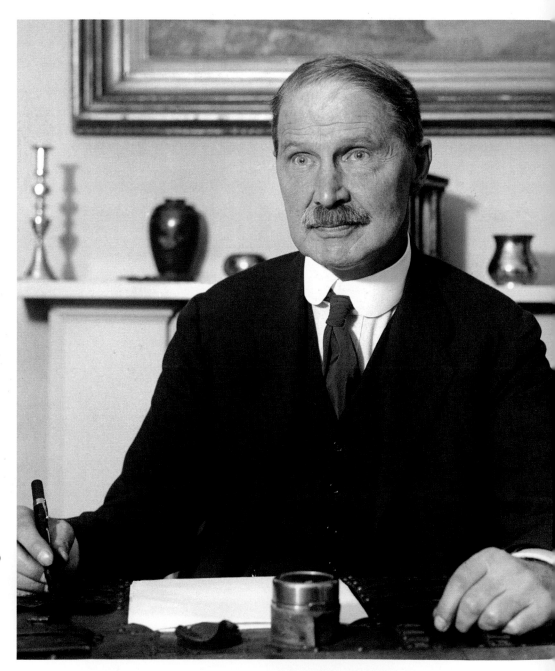

Andrew Bonar Law,
the Canadian-born,
Conservative statesman who
was British Prime Minister
between 1922-1923. He is
pictured at his desk at 24
Onslow Gardens, South
Kensington, London.
**20th October, 1922**

A portrait of Miss Partridge,
who assembles wireless
radios.
**5th November, 1922**

Crossing Guard Mr Cannell
shepherds children across
the road at Tufnell Park.
**6th November, 1922**

Mrs Grant Morden
canvasses for votes on
behalf of her husband,
who is standing as the
Conservative candidate in
the Brentford and Chiswick
by-election.
**9th November, 1922**

Labour Prime Minister Ramsay Macdonald with Welsh Labour Party MP for Caerphilly, Morgan Jones.
**22nd November, 1922**

# EDITH THOMPSON'S VERSION OF LOVE LETTERS

# The Daily Mirror

## NET SALE MUCH THE LARGEST OF ANY DAILY PICTURE NEWSPAPER

No. 5,961.    Registered at the G.P.O. as a Newspaper    **SATURDAY, DECEMBER 9, 1922**    One Penny.

## EXECUTED | PETITION | ILFORD SENSATIONS

Liam Mellows and, inset, Rory O'Connor, two of four Irish Republican leaders executed in Mountjoy Gaol, Dublin, yesterday. The executions came with doubly dramatic effect as immediately following the assassination of Brigadier Sean Hales, member of Dail Eireann.

Miss Amy Tempest, the co-respondent.

Mrs. Ellen Mary Shufflebotham, the petitioner.

Dr. Frank Shufflebotham, the respondent.

The hearing of the divorce petition brought by Mrs. Ellen M. Shufflebotham against her husband, Dr. Shufflebotham, was opened yesterday. Misconduct with a former servant, Miss Amy Tempest, is alleged and denied.

Members of the jury arriving at the court. The only woman juror in advance.

Mrs. Thompson, who was in the witness-box yesterday.

Frederick Bywaters, who declared he struck in self-defence.

### £1,000 DAMAGES IN "TAR AND WHIP" DIVORCE SUIT

Mr. Arthur Agnew, co-respondent in the divorce petition brought by Mr. William Percival Melhuish against his wife, with Mrs. Agnew. Inset, Mrs. Follett, who was charged with misconduct in a cross petition dismissed. Mr. Melhuish was granted a decree nisi.

Outside the Old Bailey at half-past three yesterday morning.—(*Daily Mirror*.)

Mrs. Thompson's evidence caused many sensations during yesterday's hearing of the Ilford murder charge at the Old Bailey. She admitted "we had talked about making my husband ill," but denied that she had ever given him anything with that intent. She appeared very ill, and many of her replies were almost inaudible.

---

Front cover of The Daily Mirror shows the extent to which the Bywaters-Thompson case captured the interest of the nation.
**9th December, 1922**

(L-R) The Duke of York Prince Albert (later George VI) and his fiancée Lady Elizabeth Bowes-Lyon (later the Queen Mother), with the Earl and Countess of Strathmore at Glamis, Scotland.
**1923**

Communist and Labour Party MP Mr. Saklatvala addresses the Six Processions meeting on 'Unemployment Sunday' in Trafalgar Square.
**7th January, 1923**

Corinthians players pictured
during a training session at
the Crystal Palace.
**10th January, 1923**

Mrs Rose Firmarger of Erith and her baby have started active training on Kentish roads for the mothers' perambulator walking race to Brighton. Mrs Firmarger's training course is a circular 30 mile route from Erith to Farnborough via Bromley, Lewisham and Greenwich.

**24th February, 1923**

King George V (L) riding in
Windsor Great Park with
his four sons: (L-R) Edward,
Prince of Wales; Albert,
Duke of York; Prince Henry;
Prince George.
**1st March, 1923**

Charlie Pringle,
Manchester City FC.
**1st March, 1923**

Princess Mary with baby
George Henry Hubert at
Chesterfield House.
**9th March, 1923**

Heather Thatcher, of 'The Cabaret Girl', listening to the wireless at home.
**10th March, 1923**

Arthur Blakiston, England.
Rugby Union, Five Nations
Championship, Scotland v
England.
**17th March, 1923**

Artist Jacob Epstein with one of his sculptures, a characteristic study of a child's head.
**21st March, 1923**

The royal family gather at Goldsborough Church, Yorkshire, after the christening of the King's grandson. (L-R) Front row: King George V, Princess Mary, Queen Mary with the baby, and Viscount Lascelles. Back row: Colonel Lane-Fox, Lady Boyne, Lady Harewood, Archbishop of York, Prince George, Lady Mary Trefusis, and the Hon. Edward Lascelles.
**25th March, 1923**

Sir Arthur Conan Doyle and
Lady Conan Doyle, with their
two sons and daughter, at
Waterloo Station, London,
before their departure for the
United States.
**28th March, 1923**

Lady Elizabeth Bowes-Lyon
(later the Queen Mother)
leaving her home in Bruton
Street, London, before
marrying the Duke of York
(later King George VI) at
Westminster Abbey.
**26th April, 1923**

The Duke and Duchess
of York leaving for their
honeymoon.
**26th April, 1923**

Bolton Wanderers goalkeeper Dick Pym (L) and teammate David Jack (R) turn away as the police try to push back the huge crowd that spilled onto the Wembley pitch before the FA Cup Final against West Ham United.

**28th April, 1923**

Facing page: The crowd swarms onto the Wembley pitch before the first FA Cup Final to be played at the Empire Stadium, only to be quelled by PC George Scorey on Billy the grey horse (top of picture).

**28th April, 1923**

The Duchess of York (later
the Queen Mother) and her
husband, the Duke of York
(later King George VI) enjoy
a game of golf during their
honeymoon at Polesden
Lacey in Surrey.
**1st May, 1923**

British Amateur Champion Roger Wethered with the trophy at Deal.
**12th May, 1923**

Queen Mary chatting to a
Girl Guide.
**19th May, 1923**

A group photograph
including the King, Queen
and Princess Mary, taken at
Aldershot.
**25th May, 1923**

Mr Stanley Baldwin at
Chequers, the premier's
official country seat.
**26th May, 1923**

J H Taylor (L) sizes up his approach shot to the sixth green at an exhibition match in Romford.
**1st June, 1923**

The Rowntree family: (L-R)
J S Rowntree, Seebohm
Rowntree, Joseph Rowntree,
Arnold Rowntree and Oscar
Rowntree.
**1st June, 1923**

Queen Alexandra, the
Dowager Empress of Russia
and Princess Victoria pass
through a Guard of Honour
of Students at the National
Rose Society's Summer
Show.
**28th June, 1923**

Lady Louise Mountbatten
with (L) Princess Theodora
of Greece and (R) Princess
Margarita of Greece,
daughters of Prince Andrew
of Greece.
**1st July, 1923**

The Prince of Wales at Guy's
Hospital: The Prince of Wales
(later King Edward VIII, then
the Duke of Windsor) with
Viscount Goschen (Treasurer
of the Hospital) and Mr M J
Waring, Vice-Chancellor of
London University.
**2nd July, 1923**

Harold Abrahams, Chairman of the British Amateur Athletics Board from 1968 to 1975, and the only British athlete ever to win an Olympic sprint championship. He is pictured here with T Campbell (L) of Yale and J W Burke of Harvard (R) at a training session for US athletes at Cambridge.

**10th July, 1923**

The Duke and Duchess of York and the Fresh Air Fund children in Epping Forest. The Duchess tries her hand at the coconuts.
**19th July, 1923**

Mrs Stanley Baldwin
declaring the League
of Nations International
Garden Fete at St Dunstan's,
Regent's Park, open.
**20th July, 1923**

Novelist and poet Thomas Hardy poses for the camera at his home, Max Gate, in Dorset during the visit of the Prince of Wales with whom he had lunch.
**21st July, 1923**

Four royal generations: the King, Queen Alexandra and Princess Mary with her baby at Marlborough House.
**28th July, 1923**

The Prince of Wales arriving
at the Boots factory in
Nottingham, during his tour
of the Midlands.
**1st August, 1923**

Surrey v Nottinghamshire at
the Oval. Notts' J Gunn is
batting.
**4th August, 1923**

Charlie Chaplin seen standing on the shoulders of Manuel Alonso, the famous Spanish tennis player, Douglas Fairbanks (L) and William T Tilden, the tennis champion.

**25th August, 1923**

Sir Gerald du Maurier, at Cannon Hall, Hampstead, with his two daughters, Jeanne and Daphne. Daphne's later fame as a novelist would eclipse that of her actor father.
**31st August, 1923**

A royal group at Balmoral
Castle. Prince George (L),
Queen Mary (second L), the
Duchess of York (second R)
and the Duke of York (R).
**9th September, 1923**

Playright George Bernard
Shaw at Muckross Abbey in
Killarney.
**20th September, 1923**

The BBC is formed to regulate the new 'radio' that was proving so popular. Pictured are George Robey and Alma Adair giving a wireless rehearsal from the Covent Garden Review 'You'd be surprised'.
**18th October, 1923**

Gladys Cooper on stage
as Peter Pan at the Adelphi
Theatre.
**3rd December, 1923**

Facing page: Mrs Hunt, who
sold apples for 40 years at
the corner of Wood Street,
Cheapside.
**25th October, 1923**

Victorious Labour candidates for the three divisions of Stepney: (L-R) Harry Gosling, John Scurr and Major Clement Richard Attlee.

**7th December, 1923**

Miners drilling into a coal-face.
1924

Coal miners having a break
to eat their meal, watched by
some of the pit ponies.
1924

A meeting of members of the Trade Union Congress General Council was held at Eccleston Square to consider the railway strike threat. Mr Ben Tillet MP arriving at the conference.
**14th January, 1924**

Ramsay MacDonald, the first British Labour Prime Minister.
**1st February, 1924**

Facing page: A crowded platform at Paddington Station, during the rail strike.
**31st January, 1924**

The Westminster (Abbey)
by-election fight begins
in earnest. Mr Churchill
(Independent Anti-Socialist)
made a statement of
his policy and started to
construct his organisation
with characteristic energy.
Mr Churchill is pictured at
his home in Sussex Square,
London.

**6th March, 1924**

The novel and artistic
'Jazz' coffee stall at the
'At Homes' of the Arts
League of Service at Robert
Street, Adelphi. Miss Edith
Sitwell and her brother
Osbert are seen taking
refreshment. The gentleman
on the extreme left is William
Walton.
**7th March, 1924**

The Bungalow Murder at
The Crumbles: the crowd
outside Hailsham Police
Court.
**7th May, 1924**

Cicely Courtneidge and her husband Jack Hulbert as rodeo artists during a theatrical garden party.
**1st June, 1924**

England v South Africa
at Birmingham. The two
captains, A E R Gilligan and
H W Taylor, tossing up.
**14th June, 1924**

The British Olympic Team marching past the Royal stand in Paris. Later dramatised in the film 'Chariots of Fire', the event saw Britain win nine gold medals.
**5th July, 1924**

The Duchess of York visits the Molesey and Hampton Court branch of the 'Lest We Forget' Association, an organisation for disabled ex-servicemen and women.
**16th July, 1924**

Great Britain's Harold
Abrahams (second R) wins
his Olympic semi-final from
USA's Charles Paddock
(second L).
**16th July, 1924**

Lady Diana Duff Cooper. In her youth considered 'the most beautiful young woman in England', she was a nurse during the First World War, a magazine editor and newspaper columnist, a stage and film actress and society hostess. She inspired characters in books by Evelyn Waugh and Nancy Mitford, among others.
**24th July, 1924**

King George V at the helm
of his racing yacht 'Britannia'.
**1st August, 1924**

Scouts parade with their
Colours passing through
the vast crowd at the Boy
Scouts Imperial Jamboree,
Wembley Stadium.
**3rd August, 1924**

Prince Henry, the Duke of Gloucester (with pipe), on manoeuvres with the Prince of Wales Hussars of 1st Cavalry Brigade at Fox Hills, Aldershot.

**27th August, 1924**

Queen Mary (L) with the Duke and Duchess of York, (later the Queen Mother and King George VI), in the rock garden at Balmoral Castle.
**18th September, 1924**

Facing page: A muffin man, making deliveries to households and announcing his presence with a hand bell.
**14th October, 1924**

John Cotter, a lucky news
vendor, who was left £450
under the will of the late
William Asch.
**14th October, 1924**

Mr and Mrs Winston
Churchill being hauled
through the streets after he
was returned as the MP for
Epping with a big majority.
**30th October, 1924**

The Dolly Sisters, Rosie and Jenny. The Hungarian-born twins lived lives of frenzied celebrity, having spent two seasons with the Ziegfield Follies before touring Europe. Famous and successful gamblers, they won $850,000 dollars in one season at Deauville. Their story was told in the 1945 film 'The Dolly Sisters', starring June Haver and Betty Grable.
**16th December, 1924**

Theatre and arts legend
Ellen Terry received the
Honour of Dame Grand
Cross of the Order of
the British Empire. Miss
Christopher St. John reading
messages of congratulation
to Dame Ellen in London.
**1925**

St James' Street, Piccadilly.
**1925**

Facing page:
Waterloo station.
**1925**

Mr John Barrymore (Hamlet) and Miss Fay Compton (Ophelia) at the Haymarket stage door, London.
**12th February, 1925**

Playwright Noel Coward
and Lilian Braithwaite leave
Waterloo Station, heading
for the United States.
**1st April, 1925**

American film star Tom
Mix with his horse at
Southampton.
**1st April, 1925**

Chancellor of the Exchequer Winston Churchill (R) playing polo for the Commons against the Lords.
**1st June, 1925**

Captain Malcolm Campbell
(in plus fours) with his 350hp
Sunbeam, at the Skegness
Motor Races, Skegness.
**9th June, 1925**

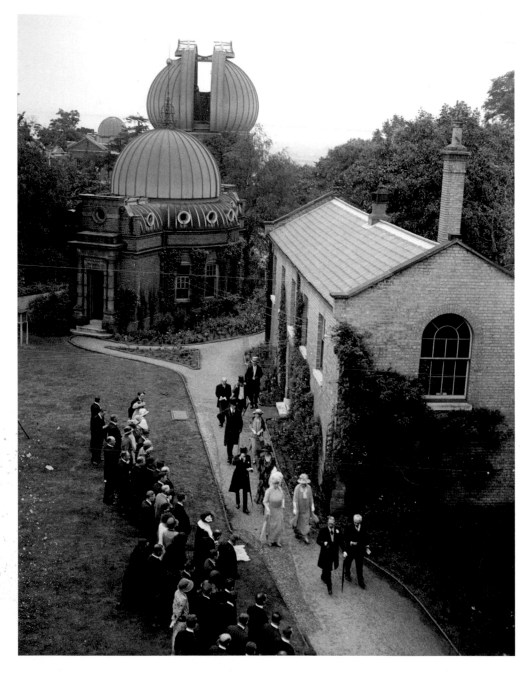

King George V and Queen
Mary in the grounds of
the Royal Observatory,
Greenwich, during a visit.
**23rd July, 1925**

Two bathers enjoy a holiday
at Cowes, Isle of Wight.
**25th July, 1925**

Facing page: A London
tram driver.
**3rd August, 1925**

Lt. Colonel Freyberg DSO, VC, being taken from the water into a rowing boat, only a quarter of a mile from the Kent coast, after an unsuccessful attempt to swim the English Channel.
**5th August, 1925**

Facing page: The Liner SS 'Majestic' sails from Southampton as planned despite a seamen's strike. The 'Majestic' was originally a German ship but was taken on by White Star Line by way of compensation for losses incurred during the First World War.
**2nd September, 1925**

Major Henry Segrave (L), with his mechanic after winning the 200 mile race at Brooklands.
**26th September, 1925**

Facing page: The start of the 200 Mile Race at Brooklands.
**26th September, 1925**

West Ham scoring the first
goal of the match against
Notts County in the first
minute of the game at
Boleyn Park.
**10th October, 1925**

Bessie Love, film actress,
on board the 'Majestic'.
**4th November, 1925**

Gloria Swanson with her husband Count de la Falaide de la Coudraye.
**26th November, 1925**

Queen Mary, King George V, Princess Victoria and other members of the royal family follow the coffin of Queen Alexandra (wife of King Edward VII). The coffin is carried by NCOs from the Grenadier Guards.
**26th November, 1925**

British troops keeping warm as
they prepare to leave Cologne
after the post First World War
occupation of the city.
**1st December, 1925**

British troops passing
through Cologne on their
way to the station at the end
of the post First World War
occupation of the city.
**2nd December, 1925**

Irving Berlin arrives in Southampton with his wife Ellin Mackay. The marriage of widower Berlin, an Orthodox Jew, and Mackay, Roman Catholic heiress to the Comstock Lode fortune, caused a sensation in American society in 1925. However, the couple remained devoted to each other for the 62 years of their marriage.

**15th January, 1926**

Harlequins' F D Field-Hyde
feeds his backs. Rugby
Union, Harlequins
v Northampton.
**30th January, 1926**

A meeting of the League of
Nations, founded in 1919.
**15th March, 1926**

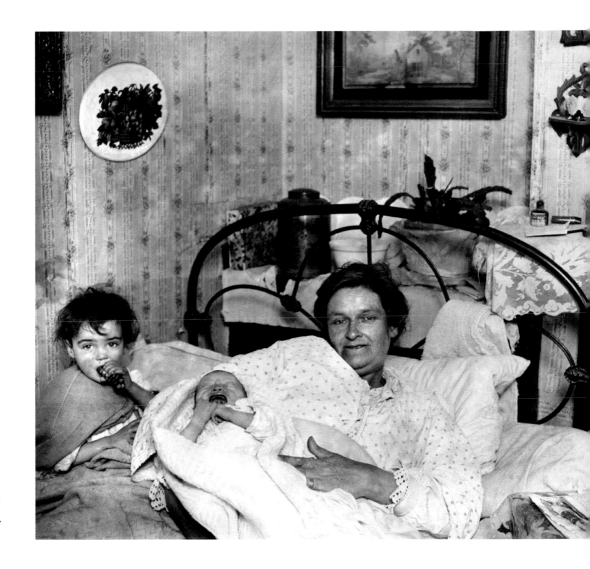

Emily Lucas of Tunbridge
Wells, with her 23rd child.
**23rd March, 1926**

Charlie Buchan,
Arsenal captain.
**1st April, 1926**

Facing page: Holidaying
in the Easter sunshine
at Eastbourne.
**3rd April, 1926**

FA Cup Final. Bolton
Wanderers v Manchester
City, Wembley Stadium.
**24th April, 1926**

The Queen Mother (then the Duchess of York) with her husband, King George VI (then the Duke of York), at the christening of their first child Elizabeth, later Queen Elizabeth II.

**1st May, 1926**

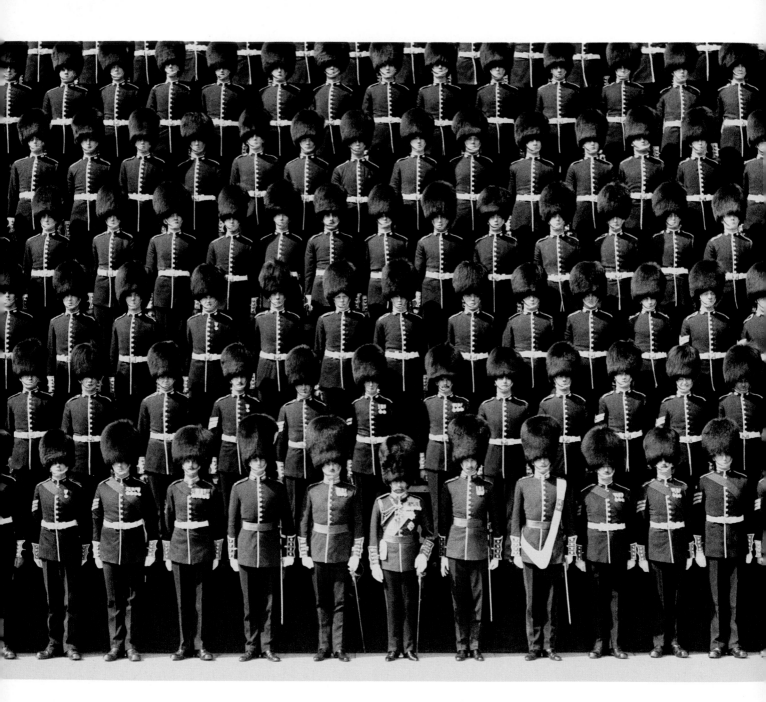

A crowd in Hyde Park during
the General Strike.
**2nd May, 1926**

Facing page: King George V
(C) with his own Company of
Grenadier Guards.
**1st May, 1926**

Broadcasting the news
during the General Strike
of 1926, at a Government
Centre for the Maintenance
of Essential Services.
**9th May, 1926**

Salvaging the last of the
German destroyers at Scapa
Flow, in the Orkney Islands.
**17th May, 1926**

The **1920s** Britain in Pictures

Captain Geoffrey de Havilland in his DH.60 Moth at the Kings Cup Air Race. De Havilland designed the highly successful Moth in 1925 with Major F B Halford: more than 3,000 were to be built and the later, Gipsy-engined, version took Amy Johnson from England to Australia at the end of the decade.

**9th July, 1926**

Facing page: Traffic returns to normal across Westminster Bridge in London following the General Strike.

**18th May, 1926**

Australia's Vic Richardson
(R) is clean bowled,
watched by England's
Harold Larwood (L) and Bert
Strudwick (C) in the Ashes
Fifth Test.
**16th August, 1926**

Facing page: Spectators
cheer wildly as the players
come out on to the pavillion
balcony at the Oval after
England won the Ashes,
defeating Australia.
**18th August, 1926**

The 'Argossy', the world's largest commercial aeroplane, a three motor double decker with seats for 18 people, on its arrival in Berlin.

**27th August, 1926**

St Kilda, the island in the outer Hebrides, whose inhabitants are short of stores owing to storms.
**3rd September, 1926**

Jessie Matthews, later to become Britain's first international film star and the 'other woman' in a nationally-reported divorce case, dubbed 'The Diva of Debauchery' by the press. Much later she emerged from showbusiness obscurity to be cast as the respectable Mrs Dale in the BBC radio series.
**6th October, 1926**

Facing page: The battle cruisers 'Repulse' and 'Renown' steaming into action with the Atlantic Fleet.
**30th October, 1926**

The New Zealand Maoris perform their haka before their match with the Harlequins.
**30th October, 1926**

A barricade on the British
bund at the Custom House,
following Nationalist riots in
Hankow, China.
**1st December, 1926**

Chancellor of the Exchequer,
Winston Churchill, inspects
the mechanised Army.
**1927**

Major Henry Segrave in 'Sunbeam', the car in which he was to break the world land speed record in March with an average speed of over 200mph.
**24th January, 1927**

The Duke and Duchess of
York aboard HMS 'Renown'
pass through the Panama
Canal.
**12th February, 1927**

Lawrence of Arabia:
T E Lawrence, author,
archaeologist and soldier,
on his Brough Superior
motorcycle during his
service with the RAF.
**26th March, 1927**

Competitors in the Gold
Bowl competing on tandems,
triplets and standard
bicycles.
**8th April, 1927**

Facing page: Aerial view of
Wembley during the FA Cup
Final, Arsenal v Cardiff City.
**23rd April, 1927**

'Tuttimen' offering oranges to
willing recipients during Hock
Tuesday at Hungerford.
**26th April, 1927**

Beating the last point on the Embankment Wall before coming ashore during the Beating the Bounds of St Clement Dane Parish.
**26th May, 1927**

An attack on the France goal during England's 6-0 win in a friendly match.
**26th May, 1927**

Captain Charles Lindbergh's Spirit of St Louis in flight during his visit to London, after his successful non-stop transatlantic flight between New York and Paris.
**28th May, 1927**

Henk Timmer in the
Wimbledon Championships.
**20th June, 1927**

Bill Voce, Nottinghamshire, during the third day of the County Championship, Surrey v Nottinghamshire, at The Oval.
**2nd August, 1927**

Thomas Mann addressing
a mass meeting in Trafalgar
Square at the time of the
'Red Scare' Sacco & Vanzetti
executions, finally carried out
after years of protests from
the likes of Mann, H G Wells
and Albert Einstein.

**7th August, 1927**

Rosslyn Park captain
Jimmy Fulljames kicks a
conversion. Rugby Union,
Harlequins v Rosslyn Park.
**10th September, 1927**

Gene Tunney and Jack
Dempsey, to meet in
Chicago to fight for the
World Heavyweight
Championship.
**14th September, 1927**

United Services' W H Wood grabs the loose ball. Rugby Union, Harlequins v United Services.
**24th September, 1927**

Writers George Bernard
Shaw, Hilaire Belloc and
G K Chesterton in a London
debate.
**29th October, 1927**

The Duke of York leaving a
'Hush-Hush' tank after taking
a ride.
**2nd November, 1927**

King George V places his
wreath at the Cenotaph on
Armistice Day.
**11th November, 1927**

King Feisul of Iraq on his
visit to the United Kingdom.
**1st December, 1927**

A day in Hyde Park.
**5th January, 1928**

Facing page: A lost charabanc was discovered by a search party, buried in the snow between Godstone and Redhill.
**30th December, 1927**

Paving blocks and stonework
thrown in all directions by
floodwater at Grosvenor
Road, London.
**7th January, 1928**

A rowing boat washed up
from the Thames into Page
Street, Westminster, by
flooding.
**7th January, 1928**

King George V shooting
at Sandringham.
**26th January, 1928**

American-born French
expatriate entertainer and
singer, Josephine Baker.
**27th January, 1928**

James Pain & Sons'
Firework factory.
**1st February, 1928**

Princess Elizabeth being
wheeled around the grounds
of her home in Piccadilly.
**1st February, 1928**

RAF flying boats
near Baghdad.
**10th February, 1928**

The Wright Brothers' historic biplane, in which man's first powered flight in a heavier-than-air machine was made, was placed on display in London Science Museum's new building. Sent to London as the result of a dispute between Orville Wright and the Smithsonian Institution, the machine would remain there for 20 years.
**12th March, 1928**

The Duchess of York (later
the Queen Mother) presents
a shamrock to the Irish
Guards.
**17th March, 1928**

Jessie Matthews in
a Noel Coward Revue.
**24th March, 1928**

The Prince of Wales on
'Miss Muffit II' jumps a
fence during the Household
Brigade Steeplechase.
**2nd April, 1928**

Mr and Mrs Henry Ford,
on holiday in England,
with Lady Astor and
the Hon W W Astor
in the grounds at Clivedo.
**14th April, 1928**

King George V leads the
Procession of Knights of the
Most Honourable Order of
the Bath to a ceremony in
Westminster Abbey.
**14th May, 1928**

Harlequins' Wavell Wakefield (C) is tackled by Old Millhillians' Edgware (R). Rugby Union, Middlesex Sevens Tournament, semi final, Harlequins v Old Millhillians.

**19th May, 1928**

Chiefs and elders line the
route at Nairobi for the
arrival of the Prince of
Wales, on a visit to Kenya.
**1st June, 1928**

Veterans of the King's African Rifles, a multi-battalion British colonial regiment raised from the various British possessions in East Africa.
**1st June, 1928**

The Prince of Wales with General Trotter, entering the paddock at the Derby.
**6th June, 1928**

The Duchess of York (later the Queen Mother) at the British Home and Hospital for Incurables, of which she became patron in 1925. She is with Matron E L Walker and resident Esther Shaw, who came to the hospital in 1923 after falling from a window on her wedding day left her paralysed from the waist down.

**27th June, 1928**

Henry 'Bunny' Austin, who was to be the last British man to reach the Men's Singles final at Wimbledon (in 1938), and the first tennis player to wear shorts.
**30th June, 1928**

Douglas Lowe breaks the
tape to win the half-mile
at the Amateur Athletics
Association Championships
at Stamford Bridge.
**7th July, 1928**

The Prince of Wales as a
trawler skipper in Grimsby.
19th July, 1928

Dame Ellen Terry shortly
before her death.
**19th July, 1928**

One of Britain's most distinguished pioneers of aviation, William Forbes-Sempill (later Lord Sempill), lands a tiny aircraft on the Thames by a three-engined Short Calcutta flying boat.

**2nd August, 1928**

The Duke of York with camp
officials in New Romney.
**7th August, 1928**

Great Britain's David, Lord
Burghley (C) powers away
from USA's Frank Cuhel (R,
silver) and Frank Morgan
Taylor (C, hidden, bronze)
to win the gold medal in the
Mens' 400m Hurdles at the
Amsterdam Olympic Games.
**10th August, 1928**

Facing page: The Aero
Wheel, adopted by
the army in Devonshire.
**1st September, 1928**

Prince George, Duke of
Kent, in California.
**20th September, 1928**

A pavement artist at work at
St Martins in the Field.
**1st October, 1928**

The new Spitalfields Market
to be opened by the King: it
took nine years to build at a
cost of £2 million.
**2nd October, 1928**

Lily Elsie and Ivor Novello
acting in 'The Truth Game' at
the Globe Theatre.
**4th October, 1928**

Boy Scouts exhibit at the
Lord Mayor's Show.
**25th October, 1928**

Although women over 30 had been allowed to vote since 1918, Universal Adult Suffrage didn't arrive until 1928. Here a group of women, between the ages of 21 and 28, trooped down to the polling station in Stepney, East London, to vote for the first time.
**1929**

Princess Elizabeth and a
drummer, during a visit to
Scotland.
**1929**

The Imperial Airways 'City
of Glasgow' leaves the new
Croydon Airport for India.
**30th January, 1929**

The Prince of Wales shakes
hands with a Mr Lindsay at
Middlestone Moor.
**1st February, 1929**

The Prince of Wales is
made welcome by miners
in Middleston Moor, County
Durham, during his tour
of the mining districts of
northern England.
**1st February, 1929**

British and Indian Police
officers move in to quell a
street disturbance during
rioting in Bombay.
**26th February, 1929**

Some of the field taking
Beecher's Brook during the
Grand National.
**22nd March, 1929**

Riders on Rotten Row,
Hyde Park.
**27th March, 1929**

Members of the Great Britain
Ryder Cup team: (L-R) back
row, Henry Cotton, Fred
Robson, Archie Compston,
Ernest Whitcombe, Stewart
Burns; front row, Aubrey
Boomer, Abe Mitchell,
captain George Duncan,
Charles Whitcombe.
**4th April, 1929**

Winston Churchill and his wife Clementine on their way to the House of Commons for the Budget.
**15th April, 1929**

Facing page: Holiday makers with their trailer caravan, solving many difficulties for those who want to see Britain.
**23rd April, 1929**

Traffic on London Bridge.
**1st May, 1929**

Facing page: The Bank
of England, The Royal
Exchange and the Mansion
House in London.
**1st May, 1929**

The nose piece of the R101 under construction at the Royal Airship Works at Cardington in Bedfordshire.
**17th May, 1929**

Facing page: Miss Helen Wills (L) leaving the American Women's Club for a presentation party at Buckingham Palace. To the left is a disabled ex-serviceman with his tray, a familiar sight in the aftermath of the Great War.
**9th May, 1929**

The Duchess of York at
an exhibition of disabled
soldiers' embroideries, at
Lowndes Square, London.
**12th June, 1929**

Jack Dunfee fills up at the
Brooklands petrol station.
**29th July, 1929**

George Bernard Shaw
at work in his revolving
sun hut. The hut could be
manipulated so that the
author could reap the benefit
of sun all day. The hut is at
Ayot St. Lawrence.
**1st August, 1929**

Clapton Orient manager
Arthur Grimsdell (second L)
talks to his players.
**26th September, 1929**

Gracie Fields handing the
cup to the winner of the
Cycle Championship for
Young Ladies at Herne Hill.
**28th September, 1929**

(L-R) L J Archer leads from
C B Bickell in the Champion
Scratch Race at Brooklands.
**5th October, 1929**

Winston Churchill wearing a Tom Mix hat near Del Monte, California, during his visit to the Monterey Peninsular.
**29th October, 1929**

A photograph taken during
the re-illumination of the
Houses of Parliament after
they had been plunged into
darkness and business
had been conducted by
candlelight.
**24th November, 1929**

Tommy Burns (L) reluctantly shakes hands with Jack Johnson (second R), who wrested the Heavyweight title from him, as Jack Dempsey (second L) and Bob Fitzsimmons (R), son of the former champ, look on.
**12th December, 1929**

Facing page: R100 nearing the mooring mast at Cardington, during its maiden voyage from the airship station at Howden in Yorkshire. Among those who worked on the construction of the R100 were designer Barnes Wallis, later the inventor of the Dambusters' 'Bouncing Bomb', and mathematician Nevil Shute Norway, more famous as Nevil Shute the author.
**12th December, 1929**

The Publishers gratefully acknowledge PA Photos, from whose extensive archive the photographs in this book have been selected. Personal copies of the photographs in this book, and many others, may be ordered online at www.prints.paphotos.com

For more information, please contact:

**Ammonite Press**

AE Publications Ltd. 166 High Street, Lewes, East Sussex, BN7 1XU, United Kingdom

Tel: 01273 488005  Fax: 01273 402866

www.ae-publications.com